How to Write World Leaders

by

Rick Lawler

MinRef Press

How to Write World Leaders

Printed and Bound in
The United States of America

First Edition

MinRef Press
8379 Langtree Way
Sacramento, CA 95823
U.S.A.

Library of Congress Cataloging-in-Publication Data

Lawler, Rick, 1949-
  How to write world leaders / by Rick Lawler.— 1st ed.
      p.   cm.
  Includes bibliographical references (p.).
  ISBN 0-9624394-0-1 : $6.95
  1. Heads of state—Directories. 2. Letter-writing—Handbooks,
manuals, etc.   I. Title
JF37.L38 1990
351.003'025—dc20   89-27317
                                                                  CIP

Dedicated to, of course, Tang Yih-Ying
and
Sara Melissa Lawler

A special thanks must be made to embassy employees who so kindly provided information and checked the accuracy of their respective nation's listing.

Contents

Foreword by Mark West V

Introduction 7

How to Use This Book 9

Letter Writing Tips 10

Keeping Your Book Current 13

Disclaimer 14

What to do if it Doesn't Work 15

Key to abbreviations 16

Leaders of Earth's Nations 17

Selected World Organizations 85

Leaders and Nations 88

References 95

About the Author 95

Foreword

When I first examined a preliminary version of this book, it struck me as an odd idea. Why a book listing names and addresses of world leaders? To whom was this book directed? What was its target audience?

This is, after all, quite a thin volume. It is not loaded down with facts and figures, essays, and many of the other things that add to the bulk of annual directories and resource tomes.

How to Write World Leaders, after much reflection, may turn out to be one of the more useful books published in recent years—for a number of very good, practical reasons.

To whom is this book directed? I've given it quite some thought, and have developed a long list (certain that you may add to it). I share part of this list below:

* Politicians.
* Government employees engaged in foreign affairs.
* Business people involved in foreign trade and commerce.
* Organizations and associations that support or oppose various causes, including environmental, human rights, political, ethnic, nationalistic, and many others.
* Libraries, of course.
* College, university, high school and elementary school libraries.
* Teachers (imagine a class project—choosing a nation and writing to the leader of that nation to propose one or another of many ideas).
* Journalists and writers.
* Religious organizations.
* Professors and students of political science, international relations and other university departments.
* Everyday citizens like you and me who have an interest in world affairs and sometimes a desire to make our opinions and ideas known to leaders of countries other than our own.

As you can readily see, the list is a long one (and by no means complete).

This book, I imagine, may create its own market as people become aware of its existence *and what you can do with it*, giving everyone who desires a voice in world affairs.

I can't imagine why someone has not thought of such a book before.

It is, quite simply, a marvelous idea. Perhaps we have not written world leaders to any great extent simply because it never occurred to us to do so. Perhaps by having the names and addresses at hand, more and more citizens of one nation will express their opinions to leaders of other nations.

What the final result of this new idea may be, I cannot begin to imagine.

Today, with this book, it's infinitely easier for individuals and groups to go right to the top. If you're upset about the destruction of the Amazon, now you can write directly to the leader of Brazil for under a half dollar. If you desire to express support for the Soviet Union's recent changes, you can now do so directly to Mr. Gorbachev.

The fact that **How to Write World Leaders** is, in effect, a targeted reference book, it excludes information you may not need (but nevertheless pay for in other books), and yet directs you to more in-depth sources of information at your local library.

I applaud the publisher for choosing an inexpensive format, and for pricing the book within the reach of virtually every library, organization and individual.

In closing, may I encourage you to express yourself. Take the first step, add your opinion to that of tens of thousands of others, and deliver that opinion directly to the doorstep, *wherever* in the world that doorstep may be.

 —Mark West
  WestMark Associates, Oct. 1989

Introduction

A long time ago, earth's peoples decided to cooperate and build a tower to heaven. God didn't particularly like this plan, and thwarted it by causing everyone to begin speaking different languages.

With no way to communicate, cooperation was virtually impossible, and the Tower of Babel was abandoned.

Today, the situation has not improved measurably. We are still a world of differing languages, customs, religions and goals.

Today however—well today the world is shrinking. The internal affairs of one nation are no longer a singular concern of that nation; those actions affect the people of many nations.

The destruction of tropical rain forests and the resultant extinction of species concern everyone on earth.

The use of chloroflurocarbons by one nation may deplete the ozone layer and cause death and destruction the world over.

Recent changes in the Soviet Union have affected almost the entire planet. A short time ago, it would have been unthinkable for Soviet military vessels and aircraft to visit U.S. military facilities. But these things have happened.

Along with millions of others around the world, I watched with dismay the violence in The People's Republic of China during the Spring of 1989. I felt the anger and a desire to *do* something—and then it occurred to me: why not write China's leaders a letter expressing my personal outrage? It was my search for a suitable address that lead to this book.

Libraries had reference materials that listed world leaders, and some of them even had addresses. But there was no concise, consistent source of information about world leaders that included mailing addresses.

And most of those reference guides are only available at libraries because of their size and expense. I wanted a small, targeted reference guide that listed world leaders, their mailing addresses, and where possible, their phone numbers.

You hold the result of my efforts. Searching the pages that follow can open the entire world to *your* ideas, *your* opinions, *your* concerns.

The world is shrinking. The planet is girdled with computer networks, electronic mail, and fax machines. Communication is instantaneous via satellite.

Engineers are developing sub-orbital, supersonic passenger aircraft capable of making transoceanic flights in just a few hours.

Yet communication is still a problem. We have too little tolerance for the customs, religions and ideas of others.

Communicating is one way to increase understanding.

As a citizen of the world, you are, no doubt becoming more and more aware of this "shrinkage." *Your* situation (and responsibility) as a citizen of a particular nation is becoming balanced by your situation (and responsibility) as a citizen of the world.

You're accustomed to communicating your opinions, ideas, feelings and protests to the leaders of your nation. Some peoples of the world have few privileges in such discourse with their nation's leaders.

Between nations, communication is largely restricted to heads of government. The average citizen seldom has ready access to the leaders of other nations.

Until now, there has been no reference that put the names *and* mailing addresses of planet earth's leaders into the hands of its people.

If you don't like what's going on somewhere in the world, fire off a letter to that nation's leader.

If you have an idea for world peace, *your* opinion can drift across the desks of the appropriate king, queen, sultan, president or prime minister.

Perhaps the most effective pressure that can be applied to a recalcitrant government is that of public opinion. And what better way to inflict public opinion than in a deluge of outraged letters from people all over the world?

A simple book of names and addresses, a compilation of information from many sources—can it be a key to better relations? Improved human rights?

Only time—and perhaps the hand of God—will tell.

How to Use This Book

How to Write World Leaders has been designed for quick reference, and allows you to easily locate the leader of a particular nation— along with his or her address.

The first part of the book consists of an alphabetical listing of all nations of the world, along with each nation's leader(s), title(s) and mailing address(es). In many cases, a phone number is also provided, and even a few FAX numbers.

Following the alphabetical listing of nations is an alphabetical listing of the leaders, cross referenced with their respective nation. You will note that in the nations listing, the leader's last name is in bold type. Not all cultures have the same surname custom as your nation. Many Asian countries, for instance, reverse the order as compared to Western nations. Thus, for the sake of clarity, we've indicated with the bold type, the leader's last name.

In instances where two nations have similar names, or different names refer to two nations, this information is noted below.

For instance, *China* actually refers to two nations: *The People's Republic of China* and *The Republic of China*. A check of the listing for "China" includes both.

Check the following:

For *Ivory Coast* see: Côte D'Ivorie.

For *Cambodia* see: Kampuchea.

For *Taiwan* see: Republic of China ("C").

For *East Germany* see: German Democratic Republic ("G").

For *West Germany* see: Federal Republic of Germany ("G").

For *North Korea* see: Democratic People's Republic of Korea ("K").

For *South Korea* see: Republic of Korea ("K").

Territories and protectorates are listed with their parent nations.

Also included in the book are a few of the more prominent international organizations, with a contact person and a mailing address.

Listed at the end of this book are some of the reference titles we used in compiling the information. In most cases, we use information verified directly by the nations themselves (or via their embassy in Washington, DC or New York City).

Letter Writing Tips

People write letters for different reasons. One is probably motivated to write a world leader by anger, a perceived injustice, a perceived brilliant idea, or some other agreement or disagreement with an action by a particular head of government.

Others prefer going "right to the top" seeking information. Some enjoy collecting autographs. Students may choose to write a world leader as a class project. Groups and organizations may wish to forward petitions or other information.

Your motivation and subject matter determines how you might approach writing a letter to a world leader. Below are some tips to help you get your point across.

Remember, in many cases, you will be corresponding with a person who does not write or speak the same language that you do, who grew up and lives in a culture different from you own, and who rules a country with laws, a political philosophy, and problems that may differ tremendously from yours. You must take all these things into consideration when you compose your letter.

* Make sure the address is copied from this book correctly. In many cases, the postal worker in the destination country does not read your language. Therefore, it's best to type the address, if at all possible.

* Current U.S. postage rates are as follows (Check your Post Office for changes—as this is being written, there are rumors of postal rate increases due in 1990):

   Canadian rates are $.30 per ounce, Mexico rates are the same as for U.S. mail.

   For other foreign countries, the rate is $.45 per *half* ounce. In most cases, two sheets of paper and a business size envelope will weigh in under a half ounce.

   Aerogrammes cost $.39 each. You cannot enclose anything inside an aerogramme.

* When writing your letter, take some time to present your thoughts politely, logically, and in simple, direct and clear language.

* If at all possible, type your letter and make sure your spelling and punctuation are correct. Often, if your letter reaches the desk of the

world leader, it will have been translated into his or her language by a staff member. A typewritten missive makes this translation much easier. For the same reasons, avoid the use of slang and expletives—they may not be known to the translator. If you can't type the letter, print neatly. Handwriting is difficult to read, no matter how excellent your penmanship, and should be avoided.

* Keep your sentences short and to the point. A short letter with a few main points is much more likely to reach its intended party than a long, rambling letter with many thoughts and points.

* Restrain your anger, if that is the purpose of your communication, no matter how well deserved. A polite, logical presentation will have more of an impact than a hysterical blast of hate. But don't hesitate to firmly state your case, express your outrage, or even demand an explanation if you feel such is warranted.

* Be aware that responses will vary. You may not receive a reply at all. Often, a reply will come from a staff member. Rarely will you receive a personal reply from the leader directly. Don't be discouraged by this—your opinions *will* most likely reach the leader regardless.

* It's also possible that your letter may get lost in transit. The efficiency of postal workers varies tremendously from country to country. Labor actions may delay your letter, political upheavals may intercept it, as may an unscrupulous postal worker who collects foreign stamps (to him or her, *your* stamps are foreign). For this reason, you may wish to use standard nondescript stamps rather than commemoratives.

* For best results, use the following format for typing or printing addresses on your envelopes:

    Name and Title of the Leader
    Office of the Leader
    Street Address or Box Number
    City and code (if any)
    COUNTRY

    For clarity's sake, the name of the country should be capitalized. If you're mailing from the United States, postal regulations require that the country be in English. Don't forget your return address both on the envelope and somewhere on the letter. If you wish to send your letter via registered mail, contact your local post office for details and costs.

* Avoid the use of form letters and those fill-in-the-blank letters and cards used by many organizations. These efforts have very little impact. An individual, personalized letter in your own words is a much better way to present your opinions. That form letter may sound polished and powerful—but it's really an indication that you don't have the determination to do your own thinking.

* Be prepared to wait. Not only is your letter subject to the whims of

11

fate and postal clerks, delivery is often excruciatingly slow. Add more time if your letter needs to be translated. A response within two months is an indication that everything went smoothly.

* Autograph collectors should avoid writing a letter that merely requests the leader's autograph. This wastes the leader's time and the time of his or her staff. Wait until you have something substantive to share. That way, if you receive a reply, the contents and the signature will be of equal interest.

* If you're writing about something of deep concern to you, don't write blind. Do some research beforehand. Reference librarians can help you to unearth information about the world leader you're intending to write. Libraries often carry foreign newspapers, which will allow you to gauge the political and social climate of the nation that interests you. The same reference materials can fill you in on the nation's economic and environmental status, its industrial, tourist and religious perspective. See the reference listing at the end of this book of examples of where to look.

* Perhaps most important of all—be persistent. If you're fighting for human rights, or environmental reasons, enlist your friends in writing letters; contact organizations with similar interests and encourage them to begin writing (not form letters, please!).

Make no mistake—public opinion has a significant impact. But it's not effective if it lies dormant and unspoken, if it never reaches the decision-makers. With **How to Write World Leaders** in hand, get your opinions in the mail.

I often wonder if it would have made a difference in China if, shortly after the massacre in 1989, the leaders of that nation had begun receiving tens of thousands of letters every day, day-in and day-out, expressing anger and outrage for their actions. There's no way to tell, of course, but I wonder . . .

Keeping Your Book Current

How to Write World Leaders is a reference book. Like virtually all such books, it will, at least in some respects, be outdated before it leaves the printing press.

Change is inevitable. Change among government leaders is constant. There is nothing that can be done about this situation. There are several things that can be done, however, that will increase the useful life of this particular volume.

Changes that occur between the time this book goes to press and the time it's shipped out will be noted on a separate "Late Changes" sheet.

While we have made every effort to confirm the accuracy of the information in this book, mistakes do occur.

Moreover, world leaders are human beings and not institutions. Leaders are voted out of office, they resign, they are assassinated, they're deposed, overthrown, and sometimes they die.

Fortunately, while leaders do change, addresses usually remain the same (unless, of course, someone opposed to that particular leader blows up the presidential palace).

It doesn't matter who is President of the United States, for instance, odds are that he or she will occupy the White House.

We have devised two methods to help you keep your copy of **How to Write World Leaders** current. Slipped into the back page of this book are a few sheets of adhesive labels.

When you become aware that the leadership of a nation has changed, either through newspaper or magazine reports, television or radio newscasts, you can type the new leader's name onto one of the labels and paste it over the name of the former leader.

By keeping aware of current affairs, you can greatly and easily extend the useful life of this book.

If you want to get the latest information on changes in world leadership, MinRef Press will maintain a current listing. All you need to do is send a self-addressed, stamped envelope along with a $1.00 processing fee. If writing from outside the United States, enclose postal reply coupons.

We'll check up to five nations per request and forward to you the current leader's name and address (by "current" we mean the latest

13

information *we* have—changes may have taken place by the time the information reaches you).

If you don't want to spend a dollar and a stamped envelope, you can utilize the same sources of information we do: news reports, public (or university) libraries, embassies, and the addresses in this book.

We plan to issue an updated edition of **How to Write World Leaders** every other year. Check the edition date at the front of this book. If it's more than two years old, you may want to order a current copy.

With these measures, your copy of **How to Write World Leaders** will maintain its usefulness much longer than the average reference book.

If a letter you write to a world leader is ever returned as undeliverable, we would like to know—write us at the address listed on the copyright page of this book. With your help, we can keep our information current.

Also, we'd like to hear about any successes you've had in communicating with world leaders (perhaps you might even send us photocopies of the letter you sent and the response, providing the content is not of an extremely personal nature).

We want **How to Write World Leaders** to be a useful book over a long period of time. We welcome your suggestions for improving subsequent editions.

Disclaimer

Considering the troubles Salman Rushdie has had from Islamic nations with the publication of his book **Satanic Verses**, I feel it's necessary to include a disclaimer.

The possibility exists (however slight) that you could get yourself into trouble when communicating with the leaders of foreign nations. The written word has the power to anger as well as appease—whether those words appear in a book or in a letter.

Therefore you need to be aware of this:

How to Write World Leaders, its authors, editors, publishers, printers, researchers, those distributing it, retail outlets and libraries will *NOT* be responsible for any trouble you get yourself into using the information in this book.

You are solely responsible for your own actions and the results of those actions. If you write the Libyans and get them mad at you, for example, you're on your own.

While we have made every effort to confirm the accuracy of the information in this book, we are not responsible for errors or omissions.

14

What to Do if It Doesn't Work

Let's say you dutifully send off a letter to a world leader, using the address supplied in this book—and months later, you get it back with that familiar finger pointing at your return address.

Your letter is undeliverable as addressed.

What happened?

There are several possibilities. The most obvious is that the wrong address was listed in this book (difficult as it may sound, we *do* make mistakes). In order to determine exactly what went wrong:

Check to make sure you copied it from the book correctly.

Check to make sure you affixed sufficient postage.

Check your local library to make sure that particular nation is not embroiled in a revolution, coup, or some other upheaval that might suspend mail service.

Check with your local post office to see if the country you're writing to is having labor problems regarding its postal delivery system.

If everything checks out, you'll have to come up with an alternative address. This involves a bit of research, and your local reference librarian can help. Some of the books you might use are listed at the end of this book.

Try writing in care of the nation's embassy. Reference books list addresses of local embassies. You'll also find listings for other governmental offices within the country you're writing. You may wish to send your letter in care of a minister of foreign affairs, perhaps, or the minister of information (and/or communication).

Countries normally have embassies in many nations. If your country does not have an embassy for the country you're writing, try writing an embassy in a third nation.

Also, while you're at it, let us know here at MinRef Press that your letter failed to get through. We'll attempt to ascertain what went wrong, and correct the situation.

15

Key to Abbreviations

Adm—Admiral
Brig-Gen—Brigadier General
Capt—Captain
Col—Colonel
Dr—Doctor
Flight-Lt—Flight Lieutenant
Gen—General
HH—His/Her Highness
HM—His/Her Majesty
HRH—His/Her Royal Highness
HSH—His/Her Serene Highness
Lt-Col—Lieutenant Colonel
Lt-Gen—Lieutenant General
Maj—Major
Maj-Gen—Major General
Ret—Retired

LEADERS OF EARTH'S NATIONS

AFGHANISTAN
Southwestern Asia

Dr. **Najibullah**, President

Office of the President
Kabul
AFGHANISTAN

Chairman (Prime Minister) of the Council of Ministers: Vacant
Char Rahi Sedarat
Kabul
AFGHANISTAN

Telephone: (93) 24355

ALBANIA
Southeastern Europe

Ramiz **Alia**, President of the Presidium of the People's Assembly

Office of the President
Tirana
ALBANIA

ALGERIA
Northern Africa

Col. **Bendjedid** Chadli, President

Présidence de la République
El-Mouradia

Algiers
ALGERIA

Telephone: 60–03–60

Kasdi **Merbah**, Prime Minister

Office of the Prime Minister
Palais du Gouvernement
Algiers
ALGERIA

Telephone: 60–23–40

ANDORRA
Western Europe

Josef Pintat **Solans**, President of Government

Office of the President
Andorra la Vella
ANDORRA

ANGOLA
Western Coast of Africa

José Eduardo dos **Santos**, President

Office of the President
Luanda
ANGOLA

ANTIGUA and BARBUDA
West Indies

Vere C. **Bird**, Sr., Prime Minister

Office of the Prime Minister
Factory Road
St. John's
ANTIGUA

ARGENTINA
South America

Carlos Saul **Menem**, President

Office of the President
Balcarce 50
1064 Buenos Aires
ARGENTINA

Telephone: (1) 46-9841

AUSTRALIA
Indian and Pacific Oceans

Robert J. L. **Hawke**, Prime Minister

Office of the Prime Minister
Edmund Barton Building
Macquarie Street
Barton ACT 2600
Canberra
AUSTRALIA

Telephone: (062) 723955

AUSTRIA
Central Europe

Dr. Kurt **Waldheim**, Federal President

Office of the President
Argentinierstrasse 20
A-1040 Vienna
AUSTRIA

Franz **Vranitzky**, Chancellor

Office of the Chancellor

Argentinierstrasse 20
A-1040 Vienna
AUSTRIA

The BAHAMAS
West Indies

Sir Lynden Oscar **Pindling**, Prime Minister

Office of the Prime Minister
P.O. Box N-3733
Rawson Sq.
Nassau
THE BAHAMAS

Telephone: 322-2805

BAHRAIN
Persian Gulf

Sheikh Isa bin Sulman al-**Khalifa**, Amir

Amiri Court
P.O. Box 555
Riffa Palace
Manama
BAHRAIN

Telephone: 661-252

Sheikh Khalifa bin Salman al-**Khalifa**, Prime Minister

Office of the Prime Minister
P.O. Box 1000
Government House
Government Road
Manama
BAHRAIN

Telephone: 262-266

Be prepared to wait for a reply. It may take several months.

BANGLADESH
Southern Asia

Hussain Muhammad **Ershad**, President

President's Secretariat
Old Sangsad Bhaban
Dhaka
BANGLADESH

Telephone: 310111-5

Moudud **Ahmed**, Prime Minister

Prime Minister's Secretariat
Sher-e-Bangla Nagar
Dhaka
BANGLADESH

Telephone: 328292

BARBADOS
West Indies

Rt. Hon. Lloyd Erskine **Sandiford**, Prime Minister

Office of the Prime Minister
Government Headquarters
Bay Street
St. Michael
BARBADOS

Telephone: 436-6435

BELGIUM
Northwestern Europe

HM King **Baudouin** I, King of the Belgians

Palais Royal
B-1000 Bruxelles
BELGIUM

21

Dr. Wilfried **Martens**, Prime Minister

Office of the Prime Minister
16 rue de la Loi
1000 Brussels
BELGIUM

Telephone: (02) 513-80-20

BELIZE
Caribbean Coast of South America

George **Price**, Prime Minister

Office of the Prime Minister
Belmopan
BELIZE

Telephone: 08-2346

PEOPLE'S REPUBLIC OF BENIN
Western Africa

Brig-Gen Mathieu **Kérékou**, President

Office of the President
BP 2028
Cotonou
BENIN

Telephone: 30-00-90

KINGDOM OF BHUTAN
Himalayas

HM Jigme Singye **Wangchuck**, King of Bhutan

Office of the King
Thimphu
BHUTAN

BOLIVIA
South America

Jaime **Paz Zamora**, President

Office of the President
Palacio de Gobierno
Plaza Murillo
La Paz
BOLIVIA

Telephone: (02) 371317

BOTSWANA
Southern Africa

Dr. Quett Ketumile Joni **Masire**, President

State House
Private Bag 001
Gaborone
BOTSWANA

Telephone: 355444

BRAZIL
Central South America

Fernando Collor de **Mello**, President

Office of the President
Palácio do Planalto
Praca dos Três Poderes
70.150 Brasília, DF
BRAZIL

Telephone: (061) 223-2714

Avoid the use of form letters and postal cards, often supplied by various organizations. Your prose might not be as polished or professional, but it will make more of an impact.

BRUNEI
Southeastern Asia

HM Sir Muda **Hassanal** Bolkiah Mu'izzaddin Waddaulah, Sultan and Yang Di-Pertuan and Prime Minister

Office of the Sultan and Prime Minister
Istana Nurul Iman
Bandar Seri Begawan
BRUNEI

Telephone: (02) 29988

BULGARIA
Southeastern Europe

Petar **Mladenov**, President of the State Council

Office of the President

Blvd. Dondukov 1
1000 Sofia
BULGARIA

Telephone: 86-91

Georgi Ivanov **Atanasov**, Chairman, Council of Ministers (Premier)

Office of the Premier
1000 Sofia
BULGARIA

BURKINA FASO
Western Africa

Capt. Blaise **Campaoré**, Chairman of the Popular Front

Office of the Chairman
Ouagadougou
BURKINA FASO

BURMA
Southeastern Asia

Gen. **Saw Maung**, Chairman, State Law & Order Restoration Council

Office of the Chairman
Ady Road
Rangoon
BURMA

Telephone: (01) 60776

U Maung Maung **Kha**, Prime Minister

Minister's Office
Rangoon
BURMA

Telephone: (01) 83742

BURUNDI
Central Africa

Maj. Pierre **Buyoya**, President

Office of the President
Bujumbura
BURUNDI

Telephone: 6063

Adrien **Sibomana**, Prime Minister

Office of the Prime Minister
Bujumbura
BURUNDI

CAMEROON
Western Coast of Africa

Paul **Biya**, President

Office of the President
Central Post Office
Yaoundé
CAMEROON

Telephone: 23-40-25

CANADA
Northern North America

(Martin) Brian **Mulroney**, Prime Minister

Office of the Prime Minister
Langevin Blk.
Ottawa, Ontario K1A 0A2
CANADA

Telephone: (613) 992-4211

CAPE VERDE
Central Atlantic Ocean

Aristides Maria **Pereira**, President

Office of the President
Presidência da República
Praia
São Tiago
CAPE VERDE

Telephone: 260

Pedro **Pires**, Prime Minister

Office of the Prime Minister
Praca 12 de Setembro
CP 16
Praia
São Tiago
CAPE VERDE

Telephone: 248

CENTRAL AFRICAN REPUBLIC
Central Africa

Gen. André-Dieudonne **Kolingba**, President and Prime Minister

Office of the President and Prime Minister
Palais de la Renaissance
Bangui
CENTRAL AFRICAN REPUBLIC

Telephone: 61-03-23

CHAD
North Central Africa

Hissein **Habré**, President

Office of the President
N'Djamena
CHAD

Telephone: 514437

CHILE
Pacific Coast of South America

Patricio **Aylwin**, President

Office of the President
Santiago
CHILE

THE PEOPLE'S REPUBLIC OF CHINA
Eastern Asia

Jiang Zemin, Chairman Communist Party

Office of the Chairman
Zhonganahai
Beijing
PEOPLE'S REPUBLIC OF CHINA

Yang Shangkun, President

Office of the President
Zhonganahai
Beijing
PEOPLE'S REPUBLIC OF CHINA

Li Peng, Premier, State Council

Office of the Premier
Zhonganahai
Beijing
PEOPLE'S REPUBLIC OF CHINA

Deng Xiaoping, Chairman, Central Military Command

Office of the Chairman
Zhonganahai
Beijing
PEOPLE'S REPUBLIC OF CHINA

REPUBLIC OF CHINA (TAIWAN)
Southeast Coast of Mainland China

Lee Teng-Hui, President

Office of the President
Chieh-Shou Hall
Chung-King South Road
Taipei
Taiwan
REPUBLIC OF CHINA

Telephone: (02) 311–3731

COLOMBIA
Northwestern South America

Dr. Virgilio **Barco** Vargas, President

Office of the President
Bogotá
COLOMBIA

THE COMOROS
Mozambique Channel

Mohamed **Djohar**, Interim Leader

Office of the President
BP 421
Moroni
THE COMOROS

Telephone: 2413

THE CONGO
Western Coast of Africa

Gen. Denis **Sassou-Nguesso**, President

Office of the President
Palais du Peuple
Brazzaville
THE CONGO

Ange-Edouard **Poungui**, Prime Minister

Office of the Prime Minister
Brazzaville
THE CONGO

COSTA RICA
Central America

Lic. Oscar Rafael **Arias** Sánchez, President

Casa Presidencial
Apdo 520
Zapote
San José
COSTA RICA

Telephone: 244092

CÔTE D'IVOIRE (The Ivory Coast)
Western Coast of Africa

Dr. Félix **Houphouët-Boigny**, President

Office of the President
Abidjan
CÔTE D'IVOIRE

CUBA
Caribbean Sea

Dr. Fidel **Castro** Ruz, President

Office of the President
Consejo de Estado
Plaza de la Revolución
Ciudad de la Habana
CUBA

CYPRUS
Eastern Mediterranean Sea

George **Vassiliou**, President

Office of the President
Presidential Palace
Nicosia
CYPRUS

CZECHOSLOVAKIA
Central Europe

Vaclav **Havel**, President

Office of the President
119 08 Praha 1-Hrad
Prague
CZECHOSLOVAKIA

Telephone: (02) 2101 or 534541

Marian **Calfa**, Prime Minister

Office of the Prime Minister
Nábr. kpt Jarose 4
125 09 Praha 1
Prague
CZECHOSLOVAKIA

Telephone: (02) 2102 or 539041

DENMARK
Northern Europe

HM Queen **Margrethe II**, Queen of Denmark

Office of the Queen
Amalienborg Palace
Copenhagen k.
DENMARK

Poul **Schlüter**, Prime Minister

Office of the Prime Minister
Christiansborg Palace
Prins Jørgens Gaard II
1218 Copenhagen k.
DENMARK

Telephone: (01) 92–33–00

Danish External Territory
GREENLAND

Jonathan **Motzeldt**, Prime Minister

Greenland Home Rule Government
P.O. Box 1015
3900 Nuuk
GREENLAND

Telephone: (009) 299–2–30–00

DJIBOUTI
Horn of Africa

Hassan Gouled Aptidon, President and Commander-in-Chief of the Armed Forces

Office of the President
Djibouti
DJIBOUTI

Barkat Gourad Hamadou, Prime Minister

Office of the Prime Minister
BP 2086
DJIBOUTI

Telephone: 351494

DOMINICA
West Indies

Sir Clarence Augustus **Seignoret**, President

Office of the President
Victoria Street
Roseau
DOMINICA

Telephone: 82054

Mary Eugenia **Charles**, Prime Minister

Office of the Prime Minister
Government Headquarters
Kennedy Avenue
Roseau
DOMINICA

Telephone: 82406

World population increases approximately 240,000 people each day. That's a net increase, counting births and subtracting deaths.

THE DOMINICAN REPUBLIC
Caribbean Sea

Dr. Joaquín **Balaguer** Ricardo, President

Office of the President
Santo Domingo
THE DOMINICAN REPUBLIC

ECUADOR
Western Coast of South America

Ing. Rodrigo **Borja** Cevallos, President

Office of the President
Palacio Nacional
Garciá Moreno 1043
Quito
ECUADOR

Telephone: 216–300

EGYPT
Northeastern Africa

Mohammed Hosni **Mubarak**, President

Office of the President
Cairo
EGYPT

Dr. Atef **Sedky**, Prime Minister

Office of the Prime Minister
Cairo
EGYPT

EL SALVADOR
Central America

(Felix) Alfredo **Cristiani** Buckard, President

Office of the President
Casa Presidencial
San Salvador
EL SALVADOR

EQUATORIAL GUINEA
Western Coast of Africa

Brig-Gen Teodoro Obiang Nquema **Mbasogo**, President

Office of the President
Malabo
EQUATORIAL GUINEA

ETHIOPIA
Eastern Africa

Lt-Col **Mengistu** Haile-Mariam, President

Office of the President
Addis Ababa
ETHIOPIA

Capt **Fikre-Selassie** Wogderess, Prime Minister

Office of the Prime Minister
P.O. Box 1013
Addis Ababa
ETHIOPIA

Telephone: 123400

FIJI
Pacific Ocean

Ratu Sir Penaia **Ganilau**, President

Office of the President
Suva
FIJI

Ratu Sir Kamisese **Mara**, Prime Minister

Office of the Prime Minister
6 Berkeley Crescent
Domain
Suva
FIJI

Telephone: 45136

FINLAND
Northern Europe

Dr. Mauno **Koivisto**, President

Office of the President
Helsinki
FINLAND

Harri **Holkeri**, Prime Minister

Prime Minister's Office
Aleksanterinkatu 30
00170 Helsinki
FINLAND

Telephone: (90) 1601

FRANCE
Western Europe

François **Mitterrand**, President

Office of the President
Palais de l'Elysée
55–57 rue du Faubourg Saint Honoré
75008 Paris
FRANCE

Telephone: (1) 42–92–81–00

Michel **Rocard**, Prime Minister

Office of the Prime Minister
57 rue de Varenne
75700 Paris
FRANCE

Telephone: (1) 45-55-95-50

FRENCH TERRITORIES
Southern Pacific Ocean

FRENCH POLYNESIA

Jean **Montpezat**, High Commissioner

High Commissioner's Office
Papeete
FRENCH POLYNESIA

Telephone: 568.42.20.00 FAX 689.42.37.18

NEW CALEDONIA

Bernard **Grasset**, High Commissioner

High Commissioner's Office
Nouméa
NEW CALEDONIA

Telephone: 687.27.28.22 FAX 687.27.28.28

GABON
Western Coast of Africa

El Hadj Omar (Albert-Bernard) **Bongo**, President

Office of the President
Libreville
GABON

Léon **Mébiame**, Prime Minister

Office of the Prime Minister
BP 546
Libreville
GABON

THE GAMBIA
Western Coast of Africa

Alhaji Sir Dawda Kairaba **Jawara**, President

Office of the President
State House
Banjul
THE GAMBIA

Telephone: 27208

THE GERMAN DEMOCRATIC REPUBLIC (GDR)
Eastern Europe

Gregor **Gysi**, Chairman; Council of State

Office of the Chairman
Marx-Engels-Platz 1
1020 Berlin
GERMAN DEMOCRATIC REPUBLIC

Hans **Modrow**, Premier

Office of the Premier
Klosterstr 47
1020 Berlin
GERMAN DEMOCRATIC REPUBLIC

FEDERAL REPUBLIC OF GERMANY (FRG)
Europe

Dr. Richard von **Weizsäcker**, Federal President
Office of the Federal President
Kaiser-Friedrich str. 16
5300 Bonn 1
FEDERAL REPUBLIC OF GERMANY

Telephone: (0228) 2001

Dr. Helmut **Kohl**, Federal Chancellor

Office of the Federal Chancellor
Bundeskanzleramt
Adenaverallee 141
5300 Bonn 1
FEDERAL REPUBLIC OF GERMANY

Telephone: (0228) 561

GHANA
Western Coast of Africa

Flight-Lt (Ret) Jerry John **Rawlings**, Chairman of the Provisional
National Defense Council

Office of the Chairman
Accra
GHANA

GREECE
Southeastern Europe

Christos **Sartzetakis**, President

Presidential Palace
7 Vas. Georgiou B' Street
Athens
GREECE

Telephone: (01) 724 8721

Tzannis **Tzannetakis**

Office of the Prime Minister
Greek Parliament
Athens
GREECE

Telephone: (01) 323 8434

GRENADA
West Indies

Herbert **Blaize**, Prime Minister

Office of the Prime Minister
St. George's
GRENADA

Telephone: 2255

GUATEMALA
Central America

Marco Vinicio **Cerezo** Arévalo, President

Office of the President
Palacio Nacional
Guatemala City
GUATEMALA

Telephone: 011-502-2-21-2-12

GUINEA
Western Coast of Africa

Gen. Lansana **Conté**, President

Office of the President
Conakry
GUINEA

Telephone: 44-11-47

GUINEA-BISSAU
Western Coast of Africa

Brig-Gen Joào Bernardo **Vieira**, Head of Government, President of
the Council of State and Commander-in-Chief of the Armed Forces

Office of the President

Bissau
GUINEA-BISSAU

GUYANA
Northern Coast of South America

Hugh Desmond **Hoyte**, President

Office of the President
New Garden Street
Georgetown
GUYANA

Telephone: 51330

Hamilton **Green**, Prime Minister

Office of the Prime Minister
Georgetown
GUYANA

HAITI
Caribbean Sea

Lt-Gen Prosper **Avril**, President

Office of the President
Palais National
Port-au-Prince
HAITI

Telephone: 2–4020

HONDURAS
Central America

Rafael Leonardo **Callejas**, President

Casa Presidencial
6a Avda
1a Calle

Tegucigalpa
HONDURAS

Telephone: 22-8287

HUNGARY
Eastern Europe

Matyas **Sueros**, Acting President

Office of the President
Budapest
HUNGARY

Miklos **Németh**, Premier, Council of Ministers

Office of the Premier
Budapest
HUNGARY

ICELAND
North Atlantic Ocean

Vigdís **Finnbogadóttir**, President

Office of the President
150 Reykjavík
ICELAND

Steingrimur **Hermannsson**, Prime Minister

Office of the Prime Minister
Stjo'rnarráoshúsio
v/Læjartorg
150 Reykjavík
ICELAND

INDIA
Asia/Middle East

Ramaswamy Iyer **Venkataraman**, President

Office of the President
Rashtrapti Bhavan
New Delhi 110004
INDIA

Telephone: (11) 3015321

V.P. **Singh**, Prime Minister

Office of the Prime Minister
South Block
New Delhi 110011
INDIA

Telephone: (11) 3012312

INDONESIA
13,700 Pacific Ocean Islands

Gen. (Ret) **Soeharto**, President

Office of the President
Istana Merdeka
Jakarta
INDONESIA

Telephone (021) 331097

IRAN
Western Asia

Ali Akbar **Hashemi-Rafsanjani**

Office of the President
Teheran
IRAN

Ali **Khamenei**, Ayatollah

Office of the Ayatollah
Teheran
IRAN

IRAQ
Western Asia

Saddam **Husayn**, President and Prime Minister

Presidential Palace
Karradat Mariam
Baghdad
IRAQ

IRELAND
North Atlantic Ocean

Dr. Patrick J. **Hillery**, President

Office of the President
'Aras an Uachtaráin
Phoenix Park
Dublin 8
IRELAND

Telephone: (01) 772815

Charles J. **Haughey**, Taoiseach (Prime Minister)

Office of An Taoiseach
Government Buildings
Upper Merrion Street
Dublin 2
IRELAND

Telephone: (01) 689333

ISRAEL
Western Asia

Gen. Chaim **Herzog**, President

Office of the President
Jerusalem
ISRAEL

Yitzhak **Shamir**, Prime Minister

Office of the Prime Minister
Hakirya
Ruppin Street
Jerusalem
ISRAEL

ITALY
Southern Europe

Francesco **Cossiga**, President of the Republic

Office of the President
Palazzo del Quirinale
00187 Rome
ITALY

Telephone: (06) 4699

Giulio **Andreotti**, Prime Minister

Office of the Prime Minister
Palazzo Chigi
Piazza Colonna 370
00100 Rome
ITALY

Telephone: (06) 6779

JAMAICA
Caribbean Sea

Michael **Manley**, Prime Minister

Office of the Prime Minister
1 Devon Road
Kingston 10
JAMAICA

Telephone: 927–9941

You can help convince world leaders—all you have to do is write.

JAPAN
Eastern Asia

Toshiki **Kaifu**, Prime Minister

Office of the Prime Minister
1-6, Nagata-cho
Chiyoda-ku
Tokyo
JAPAN

Telephone: (3) 581-2361

JORDAN
Western Asia

HM King **Hussein** Ibn Talal

Royal Palace
Amman
JORDAN

Mudar **Badran**, Prime Minister

Office of the Prime Minister
P.O. Box 80
35216 Amman
JORDAN

Telephone: 641211

KAMPUCHEA*
Southeastern Asia

Heng **Samria**, President of the Council of State

Office of the President
Phnom-Penh
KAMPUCHEA

Loss of the ozone later may render the surface of our planet uninhabitable. Ozone protects all life from damaging ultraviolet radiation.

CAMBODIA*

Norodom Sihanouk, President

Office of the President
Phnom-Penh
CAMBODIA

Son Sann, Prime Minister

Office of the Prime Minister
Phnom-Penh
CAMBODIA

* At the time of this writing, the government of Kampuchea (Cambodia) was unsettled and uncertain. Rapid changes may cause these names and addresses to be unreliable.

KENYA
Eastern Coast of Africa

Daniel arap **Moi**, President

Office of the President
Harambee House
Harambee Avenue
P.O. Box 30510
Nairobi
KENYA

Telephone: 27411

KIRIBATI
Mid-Pacific Ocean

Ieremia T. **Tabai**, President

Office of the President
P.O. Box 61
Bairiki
Tarawa

KIRIBATI

Telephone: 21342

THE DEMOCRATIC PEOPLE'S REPUBLIC OF KOREA
Asia

Marshal **Kim** Il-song, President

Office of the President
Pyongyang
NORTH KOREA

Yon Hyong-muk, Premier

Office of the Premier
Pyongyang
NORTH KOREA

REPUBLIC OF KOREA
Asia

Roh Tae-Woo, President

Office of the President
Chong Wa Dae
1 Sejong-no
Chongno-ku
Seoul
SOUTH KOREA

Kang Young Hoon, Prime Minister

Office of the Prime Minister
77 Sejong-no
Chongno-ku
Seoul
SOUTH KOREA

Telephone: 720-2001

KUWAIT
Persian Gulf

HH Sheikh Jabir al-Ahmad al-Jabir Al-**Sabah**, Amir of Kuwait

Office of the Amir
Bayan Palace
KUWAIT

Sheikh Sa'd al-Abdullah as-Salim Al-**Sabah**, Crown Prince and
Prime Minister

Office of the Prime Minister
Bayan Palace
KUWAIT

LAOS
Southeastern Asia

Phoumi Vongvichit, Acting President

Office of the President
Vientiane
LAOS

Kaysone Phomvihan, Chairman, Council of Ministers

Office of the Chairman
Vientiane
LAOS

LEBANON*
Western Asia

Elias **Hrawi**, President

Office of the President
Beruit
LEBANON

Dr. Salim al-**Huss**, Acting Prime Minister

Office of the Prime Minister
Beruit
LEBANON

* Because of the turmoil in Lebanon, it is likely that the addresses listed are unreliable.

LESOTHO
Southern Africa

HM King **Moshoeshoe** II

The Royal Palace
P.O. Box 524
Maseru
LESOTHO

Telephone: 322170

LIBERIA
Western Coast of Africa

Gen. Samuel Kanyon **Doe**, President

Office of the President
Monrovia
LIBERIA

LIBYA
Northern Africa

Col. Mu'ammar Abu Minyar al-**Qadhafi**, Revolutionary Leader

Office of the Revolutionary Leader
Tripoli
LIBYA

'Umar Mustafa al-**Muntasir**, Prime Minister

Office of the Prime Minister
Tripoli
LIBYA

LIECHTENSTEIN
Central Europe

HSH Prince **Franz** Josef II

Schloss
FL–9490 Vaduz
LIECHTENSTEIN

Hans **Brunhart**, Head of Government

Regierungsgebäude
FL–9490 Vaduz
LIECHTENSTEIN

LUXEMBOURG
Western Europe

HRH Price **Jean** Benoît Guillaume Marie Robert Louis Antoine
Adolphe Marc d'Aviano, Grand Duke

Palais Grand-Ducal
1728 Luxembourg
LUXEMBOURG

Jacques **Santer**, Prime Minister

Office of the Prime Minister
Hôtel de Bourgogne
4 rue de la Congrégation
1352 Luxembourg-Ville
LUXEMBOURG

Telephone 47–81

MADAGASCAR
Western Indian Ocean

Adm Didier **Ratsiraka**, President

Office of the President
Antananarivo
MADAGASCAR

Col Victor **Ramahatra**, Prime Minister

Office of the Prime Minister
Mahazoarivo
Antananarivo
MADAGASCAR

Telephone: 25258

MALAWI
Southern Central Africa

Dr. Hastings Kamuzu **Banda**, President

Office of the President
Private Bag 388
Capital City
Lilongwe 3
MALAWI

MALAYSIA
Southeastern Asia

AZLAN Muhibbuddin Shah ibni Sultan Yusof Izzudin, Supreme
Head of State

Office of the Supreme Head of State
Kuala Lampur
MALAYSIA

Dr. Mahathir bin **Mohamad**, Prime Minister

Office of the Prime Minister
Jalan Dato Onn
50502 Kuala Lampur
MALAYSIA

Telephone: (03) 2301957

Most of our energy comes form burning fossil fuels—a finite resource that pollutes our atmosphere and may cause a greenhouse effect.

MALDIVES
Southern Asia

Maumoon Abdul **Gayoom**, President and Head of State

The President's Office
Male' 20–05
MALDIVES

Telephone: 323701

MALI
Western Africa

Gen. Moussa **Traoré**, President

Office of the President
BP 1463
Bamako
MALI

Telephone: 22–24–61

MALTA
Southern Europe

Vincent (Censu) **Tabone**, President of the Republic

Office of the President
The Palace
Valletta
MALTA

Telephone: 221221

Dr. Edward **Fenech-Adami**, Prime Minister

Office of the Prime Minister
Auberge de Castille
Valletta
MALTA

Telephone: 623026

MAURITANIA
Northwestern Africa

Col. Maaouiya Ould Sid'Ahmed **Taya**, President of the Republic,
Chairman of the Military Committee for National Salvation and Prime
Minister

Office of the President
Présidence de la République
BP 184
Nouakchott
MAURITANIA

Telephone: 523–17

MAURITIUS
Indian Ocean

Anerood **Jugnauth**, Prime Minister

Office of the Prime Minister
Port Louis
MAURITIUS

Telephone: 011001

MEXICO
North and Central America

Carlos **Salinas** de Gortari, President

Office of the President
El Palacio Nacional
México, DF 06066
MEXICO

Telephone: (905) 515.98.36

World population has topped 5 billion, and is growing fast. The
United Nations estimates as many as 10 billion of us may be alive just
100 years from now.

53

MONACO
Western Europe

HRH Prince **Rainier** III

Office of the Prince
MC 98000
MONACO

Jean **Ausseil**, Minister of State

Office of the Minister of State
MC 98000
MONACO

MONGOLIA
Central Asia

Jambyn **Batmönh**, Chairman of the Presidium of the People's Great Hural

Office of the Chairman
Ulan Bator
MONGOLIA

MOROCCO
Northwestern Africa

HM King **Hassan** II

Office of the King
Rabat
MOROCCO

Dr. Azzedine **Laraki**, Prime Minister

Office of the Prime Minister
Rabat
MOROCCO

Remember to affix sufficient postage. If in doubt, check with your local post office.

MOZAMBIQUE
Eastern Coast of Africa

Joaquím Alberto **Chissano**, President of the Republic and Commander-in-Chief of the Armed Forces

Office of the President
Auda Julius Nyerere
Maputo
MOZAMBIQUE

Telephone: 741121

Mário da Graca **Machungo**, Prime Minister

Office of the Prime Minister
Maputo
MOZAMBIQUE

NAMIBIA*
Southwestern Africa

*Occupied by South Africa in violation of UN resolution. It is likely, at the time of this writing, that South Africa will pull out of Namibia. If so, Sam **Nujoma**, may become Namibia's leader.

Louis A. **Pienaar**, South Africa Administrator General for Namibia

Martti **Ahtissaari**, UN Representative to Namibia

Windhoek
Namibia

NAURU
Central Pacific Ocean

Hammer **DeRoburt**, President

Office of the President
NAURU

NEPAL
Asia

HM King **Birendra** Bir Bikram Shah Dev

Narayan Hiti, Royal Palace
Kathmandu
NEPAL

Marich Man Singh **Shrestha**, Prime Minister

Office of the Prime Minister
Singh Durben
Kathmandu
NEPAL

THE NETHERLANDS
Western Europe

HM Queen **Beatrix** Wilhelmina Armgard

Noordeinde 68
Postbus 30412
2500 GK The hague
THE NETHERLANDS

Telephone: 70-62-47-01

drs. Rudolph F. M. **Lubbers**, Prime Minister

Office of the Prime Minister
Binnenhof 20
P.O. Box 20001
2500 EA
The Hague
THE NETHERLANDS

Telephone: (070) 61-40-31

Destruction of the tropical rain forests will affect us all—not only in climatic changes, but in the extinction of plants and animals that are still undiscovered, many of which may provide new drugs and medical treatments.

NEW ZEALAND
Southern Pacific Ocean

Geoffrey **Palmer**, Prime Minister

Office of the Prime Minister
Executive Wing
Parliament Buildings
Wellington
NEW ZEALAND

Telephone: (04) 719998

NICARAGUA
Central America

Daniel **Ortega** Saavedra, President

Office of the President
Casa de Gobierno
Managua
NICARAGUA

NIGER
Central Africa

Brig-Gen Ali **Saibou**, President and Chairman of the Supreme
Military Council

Office of the President and Chairman
Niamey
NIGER

Telephone: 72–23–81

Oumarou **Mamane**, Prime Minister

Office of the Prime Minister
Niamey
NIGER

NIGERIA
Western Africa

Gen Ibrahim **Babangida**, President and Commander-in-Chief of the Armed Forces

Office of the President
State House
Ribadu Road
Ikoyi
Lagos
NIGERIA

NORWAY
Northern Europe

HM King **Olav** V

Slottet
Drammensvn. 1
0010 Oslo 1
NORWAY

Telephone: (2) 441920

Gro Harlem **Brundtland**, Prime Minister

Office of the Prime Minister
Akersgt 42
P.O. Box 8001
Dep. 0030
Oslo
NORWAY

Telephone: (2) 11–90–90

OMAN
South/Southeastern Arabian Peninsula

QABOOS bin Sa'id Al **Said**, Sultan and Prime Minister

Office of the Sultan and Prime Minister

P.O. Box 252
Muscat
OMAN

Telephone: 699532

PAKISTAN
Southern Asia

Ghulam **Ishaq Khan**, President

Office of the President
"AWAN-E-SADR"
Mall Road
Mayo Road Crossing
Islamabad
PAKISTAN

Telephone: (51) 820–019

Mohtarma Benazir **Bhutto**, Prime Minister

Office of the Prime Minister
Prime Minister's Secretariat
Old State Bank Building
Islamabad
PAKISTAN

PANAMA
Central America

Guillermo **Endara**, President

Palacio Presidenciál
Valija 50
Panama'1
PANAMA

Telephone: 22–0520

PAPUA NEW GUINEA
Pacific Ocean/Eastern Section of New Guinea

Rabbie **Namaliu**, Prime Minister

Office of the Prime Minister
P.O. Box 6605
Boroko
PAPUA NEW GUINEA

Telephone: 277318

PARAGUAY
Central South America

Gen. Andrés **Rodriguez** Pedotti, President

Office of the President
Palacio de Gobierno
Asuncion
PARAGUAY

PERU
Western South America

Alan **García** Pérez, President

Office of the President
Palacio de Gobierno
Plaza de Armas S/N
Lima 1
PERU

Telephone: 279264

Luis Alberto **Sanchez**, President of Ministries Cabinet

Office of the President, Ministries Cabinet
Avda. Abancay 491
Esquina jr Miroquesada
Edificio el Progreso
Piso 8

Lima 1
PERU

Telephone: 270183

THE PHILIPPINES
Western Pacific Ocean

Corazon C. **Aquino**, President

Office of the President
Malacanang Palace Compound
J. P. Laurel Sr. Street
San Miguel, Manila 1005
THE PHILIPPINES

Telephone: (02) 521-2301-10

POLAND
Eastern Europe

Gen. Wojciech **Jaruzelski**, President

Office of the President
Ul. Wiejska 4/8
oo-902 Warszawa
POLAND

Telephone: 28-70-01

Tadeusz **Mazowiecki**, Prime Minister

Office of the Prime Minister
Ul. Wiejska 4/8
oo-902 Warszawa
POLAND

PORTUGAL
Western Europe

Dr. Mário Alberto Nobre Lopes **Soares**, President

Office of the President
Presidência da República
Palácio de Belém
1300 Lisbon
PORTUGAL

Telephone: 637141

Anibal **Cavaco** Silva, Prime Minister

Office of the Prime Minister
Lisbon
PORTUGAL

QATAR
Persian Gulf

Sheikh Khalifa bin Hamad Al-**Thani**, Amir and Prime Minister

Technical Office of the Amir
P.O. Box 923
Doha
QATAR

Telephone: 415888

ROMANIA
Southeastern Europe

Ion **Iliescu**, Provisional President

Office of the President
Calea Victoriei 49–53
Bucharest
ROMANIA

Telephone: 14 81 10

Petre **Roman**, Prime Minister

Office of the Prime Minister
Str. Academiei 34

Bucharest
ROMANIA

Telephone: 15 02 00

RWANDA
Central Africa

Maj-Gen Juvénal **Habyarimana**, President

Office of the President
BP 15
Kigali
RWANDA

Telephone: 5432

SAINT KITTS and NEVIS
West Indies

Dr. Kennedy Alphonse **Simmonds**, Prime Minister

Office of the Prime Minister
P.O. Box 186
Government Headquarters
Basseterre
SAINT KITTS

Telephone: 809-465-2103

SAINT LUCIA
West Indies

John G. M. **Compton**, Prime Minister

Office of the Prime Minister
Castries
SAINT LUCIA

Telephone: 23980

SAINT VINCENT and the GRENADINES
West Indies

James F. **Mitchell**, Prime Minister

Office of the Prime Minister
Kingstown
SAINT VINCENT

Telephone: 61703

SAN MARINO
Southern Europe

Captains Regent:
Umberto **Barulli** I
Rosolino **Martelli** III

Office of the Captains Regent
San Marino
SAN MARINO

SÃO TOMÉ and PRÍNCIPE
Gulf of Guinea

Dr. Manuel Pinto da **Costa**, President and Commander-in-Chief of
the Armed Forces

Office of the President
São Tomé
SÃO TOMÉ and PRÍNCIPE

Celestino Rocha da **Costa**, Prime Minister

Office of the Prime Minister
São Tomé
SÃO TOMÉ and PRÍNCIPE

If this book is over two years old (check the copyright page), it's
probably time to order a current edition. Write to MinRef Press for
more information.

SAUDIA ARABIA
Southwestern Asia

HM King FAHD Bin Abdul Aziz AL-**Saud**
Custodian of the Two Holy Mosques

Royal Court
Riyadh 11111
SAUDIA ARABIA

SENEGAL
Western Coast of Africa

Abdou **Diouf**, President

Office of the President
ave. Roume
BP 168
Dakar
SENEGAL

Telephone: 23–10–88

SEYCHELLES
Western Indian Ocean

France Albert **René**, President

Office of the President
National House
P.O. Box 56
Victoria
SEYCHELLES

Telephone: 24041

SIERRA LEONE
Western Coast of Africa

Maj-Gen Joseph Saidv **Momoh**, President

Office of the President
Freetown
SIERRA LEONE

SINGAPORE
Southeastern Asia

Wee Kim Wee, President

Office of the President
Orchard Road
Istana
SINGAPORE 0922

Telephone: 7375522

Lee Kuan Yew, Prime Minister

Office of the Prime Minister
Istana Annexe
Istana
SINGAPORE 0923

Telephone: 7375133

SOLOMON ISLANDS
Southwestern Pacific Ocean

Solomon **Mamaloni**, Prime Minister

Office of the Prime Minister
P.O. Box G1
Honiara
Guadalcanal
SOLOMON ISLANDS

Telephone: 21863

SOMALIA
Eastern Coast of Africa

Maj-Gen **Mohamed Siad Barre**, President

Office of the President
People's Palace
Mogadishu
SOMALIA

Telephone: 723

Lt-Gen **Mohamed Ali Samantar**, Prime Minister

Office of the Prime Minister
Mogadishu
SOMALIA

SOUTH AFRICA
Southern Africa

Frederik W. **de Klerk**, State President

Office of the State President
Tuynhuys
Cape Town 8001
SOUTH AFRICA

SPAIN
Southwestern Europe

HRH King **Juan Carlos I**, King of Spain, Head of State,
Commander-in-Chief of the Armed Forces, and Head of Supreme
Council of Defense

Office of the King
Madrid
SPAIN

Felipe **González** Márquez, Prime Minister and President of the
Council

Office of the Prime Minister
Madrid
SPAIN

SRI LANKA
Southern Asia

Ranasinghe **Premadasa**, President

Office of the President
President's Secretariat
Republic Square
Colombo 1
SRI LANKA

Telephone: (1) 24801

D. B. **Wijetunge**, Prime Minister

Office of the Prime Minister
58 Sir Ernest de Silva Mawatha
Colombo 7
SRI LANKA

SUDAN
Northeastern Africa

'Umar Hasan Ahmad al-**Bashir**, Chairman, Revolutionary Leadership
Council for National Salvation and Prime Minister

Office of the Chairman and Prime Minister
Khartoum
SUDAN

Sadiq Siddiq al-**Mahdi**, Prime Minister

Office of the Prime Minister
Khartoum
SUDAN

SURINAME
Northeastern Coast of South America

Ramsewak **Shankar**, President

Office of the President

Paramaribo
SURINAME

SWAZILAND
Southern Africa

HM King **Mswati** III

The King's Office
P.O. Lobamba
SWAZILAND

Telephone: 61080

(Prince) Sotsha **Dlamini**, Prime Minister

Office of the Prime Minister
P.O. Box 395
Mbabane
SWAZILAND

Telephone: 42251

SWEDEN
Northwestern Europe

King **Carl** XIV Gustaf

Office of the King
Stockholm
SWEDEN

Ingvar **Carlsson**, Prime Minister

Office of the Prime Minister
103 33 Stockholm
SWEDEN

Telephone: (8) 763-10-00

If possible, type your letter. It's much easier to read—and translate—than printing. Don't use handwriting.

SWITZERLAND
Central Europe

Jean-Pascal **Delamuraz**, President of the Swiss Confederation

Office of the President
Federal Chancellery
Bundeshaus-West
Bundesgasse
3003 Berne
SWITZERLAND

Telephone: (031) 613727

SYRIA
Western Asia

Gen. Hafiz al-**Assad**, President

Office of the President
Damascus
SYRIA

Mahmud **Zu'bi**, Prime Minister

Office of the Prime Minister
Damascus
SYRIA

TANZANIA
Eastern Coast of Africa

Ndugu Ali Hassan **Mwinyi**, President

Office of the President
The State House
P.O. Box 9120
Dar es Salaam
TANZANIA

Telephone: 23261

70

Joseph S. **Warioba**, Prime Minister

Office of the Prime Minister
Dar es Salaam
TANZANIA

THAILAND
Southeastern Asia

HM King **Bhumibol Adulyadej**

Office of the King
Bangkok
THAILAND

Gen. Chatichai **Choonhavan**, Prime Minister

Office of the Prime Minister
Government House
Nakhon Pathom Road
Bangkok 10300
THAILAND

TOGO
Western Africa

Gen. Gnassingbé **Eyadéma**, President

Palais Présidentiel
ave de la Marina
Lome'
TOGO

Telephone: 21–27–01

TONGA
Southwestern Pacific Ocean

HM King Taufa'ahau **Tupou** IV

Office of the King

The Palace
Nukúalofa
TONGA

HRH Prince Fatafehi **Tu'ipelehake**, Prime Minister

Office of the Prime Minister
Nukúalofa
TONGA

Telephone: 21305

TRINIDAD and TOBAGO
Caribbean Sea

Noor **Hassanali**, President

Office of the President
President's House
St. Ann's
TRINIDAD and TOBAGO

Arthur Napoleon Raymond **Robinson**, Prime Minister

Office of the Prime Minister
Whitehall
29 Maraval Road
Port of Spain
TRINIDAD and TOBAGO

Telephone: 622–3141

TUNISIA
Northern Africa

Zine El Abidine **Ben Ali**, President

Palais de la Présidence
Carthage
TUNISIA

Hedi **Baccouche**, Prime Minister

Premier Ministère
Place du Gouvernement
La Kasbah, Tunis
TUNISIA

TURKEY
Southeastern Europe

Gen. Kenan **Evren**, President

Office of the President
Cumhurbaskanlugu köskü
Cankaya
Ankara
TURKEY

Turgut **Özal**, Prime Minister

Office of the Prime Minister
Basbakanlik
Bakanliklar
Ankara
TURKEY

Telephone: (4) 1186230

TUVALU
Western Pacific Ocean

Dr. Tomasi **Puapua**, Prime Minister

Office of the Prime Minister
Vaiaku
Funafuti
TUVALU

UGANDA
Central Africa

Lt-Gen Yoweri Kaguta **Museveni**, President

Office of the President
Parliament Buildings
P.O. Box 7169
Kampala
UGANDA

Telephone: 254881

Samson **Kisekka**, Prime Minister

Office of the Prime Minister
Kampala International Conference Center
P.O. Box 341
Kampala
UGANDA

Telephone: 259758

UNION OF SOVIET SOCIALIST REPUBLICS
Eastern Europe/Northern Asia

Mikhail S. **Gorbachev**, Chairman, USSR Supreme Soviet

Office of the Chairman
Staraya pl. 4
Moscow
USSR

Telephone: 206-25-11

UNITED ARAB EMIRATES
Persian Gulf

Sheikh Zayid bin Sultan Al-**Nuhayyan**, President

Office of the President
Abu Dhabi
UNITED ARAB EMIRATES

Sheikh Rashid bin Sa'id Al-**Maktum**, Prime Minister

Office of the Prime Minister

P.O. Box 899
Abu Dhabi
UNITED ARAB EMIRATES

Telephone: (2) 361555

UNITED KINGDOM

**Northwestern Europe
and other locations**

GREAT BRITIAN

HM Queen **Elizabeth** II

Buckingham Palace
SW1
ENGLAND

Margaret **Thatcher**, Prime Minister

Office of the Prime Minister
10 Downing Street
London, SW1A 2AA
ENGLAND

Telephone: (01) 270-3000

NORTHERN IRELAND

Tom **King**, Secretary of State for Northern Ireland

Office of the Secretary of State
Stormont Castle
Belfast, BT4 3ST
NORTHERN IRELAND

Telephone: (0232) 63011/2

UNITED KINGDOM CROWN DEPENDENCIES and DEPENDENT TERRITORIES

ISLE of MAN

M. R. **Walker**, Chief Minister

Office of the Chief Minister
Government House
Douglas
ISLE OF MAN

Telephone: (0624) 26262

ANGUILLA

Geoffrey Owen **Whittaker**, Governor

Office of the Governor
Government House
The Valley
ANGUILLA

Telephone: 2622 FAX: 3151

BERMUDA

Sir Desmond **Langley**, Governor and Commander-in-Chief

Office of the Governor
Government House
Hamilton
BERMUDA

Telephone: 2-3600 FAX: 53823

BRITISH VIRGIN ISLANDS

John Mark Ambrose **Herdman**, Governor

Office of the Governor
Tortola
BRITISH VIRGIN ISLANDS

Telephone: 42345 FAX: (809) 494-4435

CAYMAN ISLANDS

Alan James **Scott**, Governor

Office of the Governor
Government House BW1
Grand Cayman
CAYMAN ISLANDS

Telephone: (809) 94 97900 FAX: (809) 94 96556

FALKLAND ISLANDS

W. H. **Fullerton**, Governor

Office of the Governor
Port Stanley
FALKLAND ISLANDS

Telephone: 48-2201

GIBRALTAR

Air Chief Marshal Sir Peter **Terry**, Governor and
Commander-in-Chief

The Convent
BFPO 52
GIBRALTAR

Telephone: 75908 FAX: 76396

HONG KONG

Sir David Clive **Wilson**, Governor

Office of the Governor
Government House

Central
HONG KONG

Telephone: 5-232031 FAX: 010 852 5 8450995

UNITED STATES OF AMERICA
Central North America

George Herbert Walker **Bush**, President

Office of the President
The White House
1600 Pennsylvania Avenue
Washington, DC 20500
USA

Telephone: (202) 456-1414

Members of Congress
U.S. Senate
Washington, DC 20510
USA

Members of Congress
House of Representatives
Washington, DC 20515
USA

U.S. TERRITORIES

AMERICAN SAMOA

Peter Tale **Coleman**, Governor

Office of the Governor
Pago Pago
AMERICAN SAMOA 96799

Telephone: (684) 633-4116

Your local library has a wealth of information available; ask the reference librarian for books about foreign nations and governments.

GUAM

Joseph F. **Ada**, Governor

Office of the Governor
Agaña
GUAM 96910

MARSHALL ISLANDS

Amata **Kabua**, President

Office of the President
Majuro
MARSHALL ISLANDS, MH96960

FEDERATED STATES OF MICRONESIA

John R. **Haglelgam**, President

Office of the President
Kolonia, Pohnpei
Eastern Caroline Islands
MICRONESIA, FM96943

NORTHERN MARIANA ISLANDS

Pedro T. **Tenorio**, Governor

Office of the Governor
Saipan
NORTHERN MARIANA ISLANDS, MP96950

PUERTO RICO

Rafael **Hernández** Colon, Governor

Office of the Governor
Box 82 Laforteleza
San Juan
PUERTO RICO 00901

U.S. VIRGIN ISLANDS

Alexander A. **Farrelly**, Governor

Office of the Governor
Government House
St. Thomas
U.S. VIRGIN ISLANDS, VI00801

Telephone: (809) 774-0001

URUGUAY
Southeastern Coast of South America

Luis **Lacalle**, President

Office of the President
Edif. Libertad
Montevideo
URUGUAY

Telephone: 989310

VANUATU
Southwestern Pacific Ocean

Fred **Timakata**, President

Office of the President
Port Vila
VANUATU

Fr. Walter Hadye **Lini**, Prime Minister

Office of the Prime Minister
P.O. Box 110
Port Vila
VANUATU

Telephone: 2413

THE VATICAN CITY
Within City of Rome

His Holiness **Pope John Paul** II

Apostolic Palace
00120 Vatican City
THE VATICAN CITY

VENEZUELA
Northern Coast of South America

Carlos Andrés **Perez**, President

Office of the President
Palacio de Miraflores
Caracas
VENEZUELA

VIETNAM
Southeastern Asia

Le Quang Dao, Chairman, National Assembly

Office of the Chairman, National Assembly
Hanoi
VIETNAM

Vo Chi Cong, Chairman of the Council

Office of the Chairman of the Council
Hanoi
VIETNAM

WESTERN SAMOA
Southern Pacific Ocean

HH Malietoa **Tanumafili** II, O le Ao o Malo

Office of the O le Ao o Malo
Apia

WESTERN SAMOA

Tofilau **Eti**, Prime Minister

Office of the Prime Minister
P.O. Box 193
Apia
WESTERN SAMOA

Telephone: 21500

THE YEMEN ARAB REPUBLIC
Southwestern Arabian Pinensula

Col. Ali Abdullah **Salih**, President

Office of the President
San'a
YEMEN ARAB REPUBLIC

Dr. Abd al-Aziz **Abd al-Ghani**, Prime Minister

Office of the Prime Minister
San'a
YEMEN ARAB REPUBLIC

THE PEOPLE'S DEMOCRATIC REPUBLIC OF YEMEN
South Shore of Arabian Pinensula

Haydar Abu Bakr al-'**Attas**, Chairman, Supreme People's Council
Presidium

Office of the Chairman, Council Presidium
Aden
PEOPLE'S DEMOCRATIC REPUBLIC OF YEMEN

Dr. Yasin Said **Nu'man**, Chairman, Council of Ministers

Office of the Chairman, Council of Ministers
Aden
PEOPLE'S DEMOCRATIC REPUBLIC OF YEMEN

YUGOSLAVIA
Southeastern Europe

Janez **Drnovsek**, President

Office of the President
Palata Federacije
Bul. Lenjina 2
11070 Novi Benograd
YUGOSLAVIA

Telephone (011) 334-281

ZAIRE
Central Africa

Marshal **Mobutu** Sese Seko Wa Za Banga, President

Office of the President
Mont Ngaliema
Kinshasa
ZAIRE

Telephone: 31312

Kengo wa Dondo, Prime Minister

Office of the Prime Minister
Kinshasa
ZAIRE

ZAMBIA
Southern Central Africa

Dr. Kenneth David **Kaunda**, President

Office of the President
State House
P.O. Box 135
Lusaka
ZAMBIA

Kebby S. K. **Musokotwane**, Prime Minister

Office of the Prime Minister
P.O. Box 30208
Lusaka
ZAMBIA

Telephone: 218282

ZIMBABWE
Southern Africa

Robert Gabriel **Mugabe**, Executive President

Office of the Executive President
P.O. Box 368
Harare
ZIMBABWE

Telephone: 726666

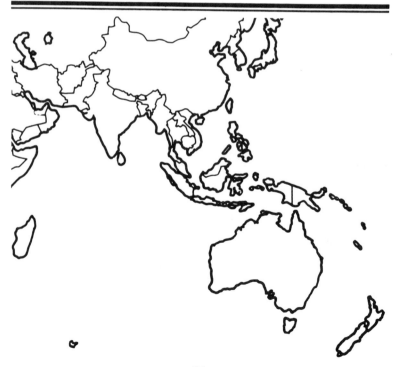

LEADERS OF SELECTED WORLD ORGANIZATIONS

UNITED NATIONS

Javier Pérez de **Cuéllar**, Secretary General

The United Nations
United Nations Building
New York, NY 10017
U.S.A.

Telephone: (212) 754-5012

Other United Nations Addresses:
Palais des Nations
1211 Geneva 10
SWITZERLAND

Telephone: (022) 310211

Vienna International Centre
P.O. Box 500
1400 Vienna
AUSTRIA

THE COMMONWEALTH

Sir Shridath S. **Ramphal** (Guyana), Secretary General

The Commonwealth
Commonwealth Secretariat
Marlborough House
Pall Mall
London SW1Y 5HX
ENGLAND

Telephone: (01) 839-3411 FAX: (01) 930 0827

INTERNATIONAL OLYMPIC COMMITTEE

Me Francois **Carrard**, General Director

Office of the General Director
International Olympic Committee
Château de Vidy
1007 Lausanne
SWITZERLAND

Telephone: 25.32.71 FAX 24.15.52

NORTH ATLANTIC TREATY ORGANIZATION (NATO)

Manfred **Wörner**, Secretary General (GE)

Office of the Secretary General
North Atlantic Treaty Organization
1110 Brussels
BELGIUM

Telephone: (02) 728 4917

ORGANIZATION FOR AFRICAN UNITY

Dr. Kenneth **Kaunda**, Chairman (Zambia)

Office of the Chairman
Organization for African Unity
P.O. Box 3243
Addis Ababa
ETHIOPIA

Telephone: 157700

ORGANIZATION OF AMERICAN STATES (OAS)

João Clemente Baena **Soares**, Secretary General (Brazil)

Office of the Secretary General
Organization of American States
1889 F Street NW
Washington, DC 20006
USA

ORGANIZATION OF THE PETROLEUM EXPORTING COUNTRIES (OPEC)

HE Dr. **Subroto**, Secretary General

Office of the Secretary General
Organization of Petroleum Exporting Countries
Obere Donaustrasse 93
1020 Vienna
AUSTRIA

Telephone: (0222) 21-11-20

THE WARSAW TREATY OF FRIENDSHIP, COOPERATION and MUTUAL ASSISTANCE—THE WARSAW PACT

Marshal Viktor G. **Kulikov**, Commander-in-Chief (USSR)

Office of the Secretary General
The Warsaw Pact
Moscow
USSR

WORLD COUNCIL OF CHURCHES

Rev. Dr. Heinz Joachim **Held**, Central Committee Moderator (FRG)

Office of the Moderator
World Council of Churches
150 route de Ferney
P.O. Box 2100
1211 Geneva 2
SWITZERLAND

Telephone: (0511) 71 11-25

LEADERS AND NATIONS

Abd al-Ghani, Dr. Abd al-Aziz; Yemen Arab Republic
Ada, Joseph F.; Guam
Ahmed, Moudud; Bangladesh
Ahtissaari, Martti; Namibia
Alanis, Dr. Joan Marti; Andorra
Alia, Ramiz; Albania
Andreotti, Giulio; Italy
Aquino, Corazon C.; The Philippines
Arias Sánchez, Lic. Oscar; Costa Rica
Al-Assad, Gen. Hafiz; Syria
Atanasov, Georgi Ivanov; Bulgaria
al-**Attas**, Haydar Abu Bakr; People's Democratic Republic of Yemen
Ausseil, Jean; Monaco
Avril, Lt-Gen Prosper; Haiti
Aylwin, Patricio; Chile
AZLAN Muhibbuddin Shah ibni Sultan Yusof Izzudin; Malaysia
Babangida, Gen. Ibrahim; Nigeria
Baccouche, Hedi; Tunisia
Badran, Mudar; Jordan
Balaguer Ricardo, Dr. Joaquín; The Dominican Republic
Banda, Dr. Hastings Kamuzu; Malawi
Barco Vargas, Dr. Virgilio; Colombia
Barkat Gourad Hamadou; Djibouti
Barulli I, Umberto; San Marino
al-**Bashir**, 'Umar Hasan Ahmad; Sudan
Batmönh, Jambyn; Mongolia
Baudouin I, HM King; Belgium
Beatrix Wilhelmina Armgard, HM Queen; The Netherlands
Ben Ali, Zine El Abidine; Tunisia
Bendjedid Chadli, Col.; Algeria
Bhumibol Adulyadej, HM King; Thailand
Bhutto, Mohtarma Benazir; Pakistan
Bird, Vere C., Sr.; Antigua and Barbuda
Birendra Bir Bikram Shah Dev, HM King; Nepal
Biya, Paul; Cameroon
Blaize, Herbert; Grenada

Bongo, El Hadj Omar (Albert-Bernard); Gabon
Borja Cevallos, Ing. Rodrigo; Ecuador
Brundtland, Gro Harlem; Norway
Brunhart, Hans; Liechtenstein
Bush, George Herbert Walker; United States of America
Buyoya, Maj. Pierre; Burundi
Calfa, Marian; Czechoslovakia
Callejas, Rafael Leonardo; Honduras
Campaoré, Capt. Blaise; Burkina Faso
Carl XIV Gustaf, King; Sweden
Carlsson, Bernt; Namibia
Carlsson, Ingvar; Sweden
Carrard, François; International Olympic Committee
Castro Ruz, Dr. Fidel; Cuba
Cavaco Silva, Anibal; Portugal
Cerezo, Arévalo; Guatemala
Charles, Mary Eugenia; Dominica
Chissano, Joaquím Alberto; Mozambique
Choonhavan, Gen. Chatichai; Thailand
Coleman, Peter Tale; American Samoa
Compton, John G. M.; St. Lucia
Conté, Gen. Lansana; Guinea
Cossiga, Francesco; Italy
Costa, Celestino Rocha da; São Tomé and Príncipe
Costa, Dr. Manuel Pinto da; São Tomé and Príncipe
Cristiani, (Felix) Alfredo; El Salvador
Cuéllar, Javier Pérez de; United Nations
Delamuraz, Jean-Pascal; Switzerland
Deng Xiaoping; PR China
DeRoburt, Hammer; Nauru
Diouf, Abdou; Senegal
Djohar, Mohamed; The Comoros
Dlamini (Prince) Sotsha; Swaziland
Doe, Gen. Samuel Kanyon; Liberia
Drnovsek, Janez; Yugoslavia
Elizabeth II, HM Queen; Great Britian
Endara, Guillermo; Panama
Ershad, Hussain Muhammad; Bangladesh
Eti, Tofilau; Western Samoa
Evren, Gen. Kenan; Turkey
Eyadéma, Gen. Gnassingbé; Togo
Farrelly, Alexander A.; U.S. Virgin Islands
Fenech-Adami, Dr. Edward; Malta

Fikre-Selassie Wogderess, Capt.; Ethiopia
Finnbogadóttir, Vigdís; Iceland
Franz Josef II, Prince; Liechtenstein
Ganilau, Ratu Sir Penaia; Fiji
García Pérez, Alan; Peru
Gayoom, Maumoon Abdul; Maldives
González Márquez, Felipe; Spain
Gorbachev, Mikhail S.; USSR
Grasset, Bernard; New Caledonia
Green, Hamilton; Guyana
Gysi, Gregor; East Germany
Habré, Hissein; Chad
Habyarimana, Maj-Gen Juvénal; Rwanda
Haglelgam, John R.; Federated States of Micronesia
Hashemi-Rafsanjani, Ali Akbar; Iran
Hassan Gouled Aptidon; Djibouti
Hassan II, HM King; Morocco
Hassanal Bolkiah Mu'izzaddin Waddaulah, HM Sir Muda; Brunei
Hassanali, Noor; Trinidad and Tobago
Haughey, Charles J.; Ireland
Havel, Vaclav; Czechoslovakia
Hawke, Robert J. L.; Australia
Held, Rev. Dr. Heinz Joachim; WCC
Herdman, John Mark Ambrose; British Virgin Islands
Hermannsson, Steingrimur; Iceland
Hernández Colon, Rafael; Puerto Rico
Herzog, Gen. Chaim; Israel
Hillery, Dr. Patrick J.; Ireland
Holkeri, Harri; Finland
Houphouët-Boigny, Dr. Félix; Côte D'ivorie
Hoyte, Hugh Desmond; Guyana
Hrawi, Elias; Lebanon
Husayn, Saddam; Iraq
al-**Huss**, Dr. Salim; Lebanon
Hussein Ibn Talal, HM King; Jordan
Iliescu, Ion; Romania
Ishaq Khan, Ghulam; Pakistan
Jaruzelski, Gen. Wojciech; Poland
Jawara, Alhaji Sir Dawda Kairaba; The Gambia
Jean Benoît Guillaume, HRH Prince; Luxembourg
Jewkes, Gordon Wesley; Falkland Islands
Jiang, Zemin; PR China
Juan Carlos I, HRH King; Spain
Jugnauth, Anerood; Mauritius

Kabua, Amata; Marshall Islands
Kaifu, Toshiki; Japan
Kang Young Hoon; South Korea
Kaunda, Dr. Kenneth David; Zambia
Kaunda, Dr. Kenneth; Org. for African Unity
Kaysone Phomuihan; Laos
Kengo wa Dondo; Zaire
Keshtmand, Soltan Ali; Afghanistan
Kérékou, Brig-Gen Mathieu; PR Benin
Kha, U Maung Maung; Burma
al-**Khalifa**, Sheikh Isa bin Sulman; Bahrain
al-**Khalifa**, Sheikh Khalifa bin Salman; Bahrain
Khamenei, Ali; Iran
Kim Il-song, Marshal; North Korea
King, Tom; Northern Ireland
Kisekka, Samson; Uganda
Kiszczak, Gen. Czeslaw; Poland
Kohl, Dr. Helmut; West Germany
Koivisto, Dr. Mauno; Finland
Kolingba, Gen André-Dieudonne; Central African Republic
Kulikov, Marshal Viktor G.; Warsaw Pact
Lacalle, Luis; Uruguay
Langley, Sir Desmond; Bermuda
Laraki, Dr. Azzedine; Morocco
Le Quang Dao; Vietnam
Lee Kuan Yew; Singapore
Lee Teng-Hui; Republic of China
Li Peng; PR China
Lini, Fr. Walter Hadye; Vanuatu
Lubbers, drs. Rudolph F. M.; The Netherlands
Machungo, Mário da Graça; Mozambique
al-**Mahdi**, Sadiq Siddiq; Sudan
Al-**Maktum**, Sheikh Rashid bin Sa'id; United Arab Emirates
Mamaloni, Solomon; Solomon Islands
Mamane, Oumarou; Niger
Manley, Michael; Jamaica
Mara, Ratu Sir Kamisese; Fiji
Margrethe II, HM Queen; Denmark
Martelli III, Rosolino; San Marino
Martens, Dr. Wilfried; Belgium
Masire, Dr. Quett Ketumile Joni; Botswana
Mbasogo, Birg-Gen Teodoro Obiang Nquema; Equatorial Guinea
Mello, Fernando Collor de; Brazil
Menem, Carlos Saul; Argentina

Mengistu Haile-Mariam, Lt-Col; Ethiopia
Merbah, Kasdi; Algeria
Mébiame, Léon; Gabon
Mitchell, James F.; St. Vincent
Mitterrand, François; France
Mladeñov, Petar; Bulgaria
Moawad, Rene; Lebanon
Mobutu Sese Seko Wa Za Banga, Marshal; Zaire
Modrow, Hans; East Germany
Mohamad, Dr. Mahathir bin; Malaysia
Mohamed Ali Samantar, Lt-Col; Somalia
Mohamed Siad Barre, Maj-Gen; Somalia
Moi, Daniel arap; Kenya
Momoh, Maj-Gen Joseph Saidv; Sierra Leone
Montpezat, Jean; French Polynesia
Moshoeshoe II, HM King; Lesotho
Motzeldt, Jonathan; Greenland
Mswati III, HM King; Swaziland
Mubarak, Mohammed Hosni; Egypt
Mugabe, Robert Gabriel; Zimbabwe
Mulroney, (Martin) Brian; Canada
al-**Muntasir**, 'Umar Mustafa; Libya
Museveni, Lt-Gen Yoweri Kaguta; Uganda
Musokotwane, Kebby S. K.; Zambia
Mwinyi, Ndugu Ali Hassan; Tanzania
Najibullah, Dr.; Afghanistan
Namaliu, Rabbie; Papua New Guinea
Németh, Miklós; Hungary
Norodom Sihanouk; Cambodia
Al-**Nuhayyan**, Sheikh Zayid bin Sultan; United Arab Emirates
Nujoma, Sam; Namibia
Nu'man, Dr. Yasin Said; People's Democratic Republic of Yemen
Olav V, King; Norway
Ortega Saavedra, Daniel; Nicaragua
Özal, Turgut; Turkey
Palmer, Geoffrey; New Zealand
Paz Estenssoro, Dr. Victor; Bolivia
Pereira, Aristides Maria; Cape Verde
Perez, Carlos Andrés; Venezuela
Phoumi Vongvichit; Laos
Pienaar, Louis A.; Namibia
Pindling, Sir Lynden Oscar; The Bahamas·
Pires, Pedro; Cape Verde
Pope John Paul II, His Holiness; Vatican City

Poungui, Ange-Edouard; The Congo
Premadasa, Ranasinghe; Sri Lanka
Price, George; Belize
Puapua, Dr. Tomasi; Tuvalu
al-**Qadhafi**, Col. Mu'ammar Abu Minyar; Libya
Rainier III, HRH Prince; Monaco
Ramahatra, Col Victor; Madagascar
Ramphal, Sir Shridath S.; The Commonwealth
Ratsiraka, Adm. Didier; Madagascar
Rawlings, Flight-Lt (Ret.) Jerry; Ghana
René, France Albert; Seychelles
Robinson, Arthur Napoleon Raymond; Trinidad and Tobago
Rocard, Michel; France
Rodriguez, Francisco; Panama
Rodriguez Pedotti, Gen. Andrés; Paraguay
Roh Tae-Woo; South Korea
Roman, Petre; Romania
Al-**Sabah**, HH Sheikh Jabir al-Ahmad al-Jabir; Kuwait
Al-**Sabah**, Sheikh Sa'd al-Abdullah as-Salim; Kuwait
Saibou, Brig-Gen Ali; Niger
Said, QABOOS bin Sa'id Al; Oman
Salih, Col. Ali Abdullah; Yemen Arab Republic
Salinas de Gortari, Carlos; Mexico
Samria, Heng; Kampuchea
Sanchez, Luis Alberto; Peru
Sandiford, Rt. Hon. Lloyd Erskine; Barbados
Santer, Jacques; Luxembourg
Santos, José Eduardo dos; Angola
Sartzetakis, Christos; Greece
Sassou-Nguesso, Gen. Denis; The Congo
Al-**Saud**, King FAHD Bin Abdul Aziz; Saudia Arabia
Saw Maung, Gen.; Burma
Schlüter, Poul; Denmark
Scott, Alan James; Cayman Islands
Sedky, Dr. Atef; Egypt
Seignoret, Sir Clarence Augustus; Dominica
Shamir, Yitzhak; Israel
Shankar, Ramsewak; Suriname
Shrestha, Marich Man Singh; Nepal
Sibomana, Adrien; Burundi
Simmonds, Dr. Kennedy Alphonse; St. Kitts and Nevis
Singh, V.P.; India
Soares, João Clemente Baena; OAS
Soares, Dr. Mário Alberto Nobre Lopes; Portugal
Soeharto, Gen. (Ret); Indonesia

Solans, Josef Pintat; Andorra
Son Sann; Cambodia
Subroto, HE Dr.; OPEC
Sueros, Matyas; Hungary
Tabai, Ieremia T.; Kiribati
Tabone, Vincent (Censu); Malta
Tanumafili II, HH Malietoa; Western Samoa
Taya, Col. Maaouiya Ould Sid'Ahmed; Mauritania
Tenorio, Pedro T.; Northern Mariana Islands
Terry, Air Chief Marshal Sir Peter; Gibralter
Al-Thani, Sheikh Khalifa bin Hamad; Qatar
Thatcher, Margaret; Great Britian
Timakata, Fred; Vanuatu
Traoré, Gen. Moussa; Mali
Tupou IV, HM King Taufa'ahau; Tonga
Tu'ipelehake, HRH Prince Fatafehi; Tonga
Tzannetakis, Tzannis; Greece
Vassiliou, George; Cyprus
Venkataraman, Ramaswamy Iyer; India
Vieira, Brig-Gen Joào Bernardo; Guinea-Bissau
Vo Chi Cong; Vietnam
Vranitzky, Franz; Austria
Waldheim, Dr. Kurt; Austria
Walker, M. R.; Isle of Man
Wangchuck, HM Jigme Singye; Bhutan
Warioba, Joseph S.; Tanzania
Wee Kim Wee; Singapore
Weizsäcker, Dr. Richard von; West Germany
Whittaker, Geoffrey Owen; Anguilla
Wijetunge, D. B.; Sri Lanka
Wilson, Sir David Clive; Hong Kong
Wörner, Manfred; NATO
Yang Shangkun; PR China
Yon, Hyong-muk; North Korea
Zu'bi, Mahmud; Syria

About the Author

Rick Lawler is an avid letter-writer, has been all his life. This week he's already fired off letters to the police chief of the city where he lives, to the president of a national company, and to the letters page of the local newspaper. He received a reply to a letter he'd recently written to his congressman.

The author of **How to Write World Leaders** met his wife through the mails in a long-distance relationship between California and Taiwan. Almost a year after that first, halting written communication, Rick flew to Taiwan and the couple were married. Alice joined him in California a few months later—and that was almost nine years ago.

Rick Lawler is a former newspaper editor, and is currently a freelance writer. His articles have appeared in *Westways, Young World, General Aviation News, Sales and Marketing Management, The Business Journal*, and others. His fiction has been published in *Pulphouse, Mature Years, Space and Time, Ellipsis . . ., Gas*, and others. Rick is employed by the University of California at Davis. He lives in Sacramento with his wife, Alice Tang Lawler, and their newborn baby.

Rick is a member of the Authors Guild and National Writers Club.

He is working on several other book manuscripts, including **MYTH: The Extinction Factor** and a novel, **The Last Barbarian**. He is completing research on a scholarly work, **The History of the Ku Klux Klan in California, 1922**.

He has won several awards as an amateur photographer, and he collects historic newspapers as a hobby.

He believes in the power of the written word and in the power of public opinion.

References

The following books and materials were utilized in the preparation of this book. Most of these books are available at your local library at the reference desk.

Europa Year Book, 1988, A World Survey, Volumes I and II, Europa Publications Limited, London, England, 1988.

The Statesman's Handbook 1989–90, Edited by John Paxton, MacMillan Press, LTD, London, England, 1989.

Who's Who 1989, A&C Black, London, England, 1989.

Chiefs of State and Cabinet Members of Foreign Governments, published Feb., April, June, Aug., Oct. and Dec. by Central Intelligence Agency, U.S. Government (edition used, July/Aug. 1989).

Foreign Consular Offices in the United States, Department of State Publication 7846, Rev. March 1989.

ORDER FORM
Use this form to order additional copies of

How to Write World Leaders
by
Rick Lawler

Order extra copies as gifts, for co-workers and colleagues, for all those people who keep borrowing your copy

All copies come with a 10-day Money Back Guarantee—if you're not satisfied with *How to Write World Leaders*, simply return it in its original condition for a full refund.

Send orders to:
MinRef Press
8379 Langtree Way
Sacramento, CA 95823

Price: $6.95 each
(Calif. residents add $.45 per copy sales tax)

Name (please print)

_____

Address

_____

City   State   Zip

_____

Please write for quantity discounts

Please allow four to six weeks for delivery